Welcome

NAOMI STARKEY

When you think of the word 'wilderness', what comes to mind? Many people will think of a dry landscape with scrubby bushes and rocks, the kind of Middle Eastern wilderness where Jesus was tempted and the Israelites wandered. Or they may conjure up Lawrence of Arabia-style rolling sand dunes, with a hint of palm trees in the distance. Alternatively (as shown on the back cover of this issue) a few may imagine the kind of icy waste found in the world's polar regions, as inhospitable as any hot desert.

Venturing into the wilderness is a challenge, whatever the climate. For some, the prospect makes them grab backpack and walking boots and set out immediately, while others will run screaming in the other direction—straight to the nearest travel agent to book a luxury hotel!

Joking aside, a spiritual 'wilderness experience' may be one that we find ourselves enduring, whether or not we feel remotely equipped to do so. 'Wildernesses of the heart' are emotionally inhospitable places where we may find ourselves wandering with no prospect of a way out.

In this *Quiet Spaces*, we will think about 'wilderness' both as a place where God may call us to adventure and also as a time of daunting, even overwhelming, difficulty. Running throughout—the path through the desert, if you like—is the message that no matter how bleak a place or situation may be, God promises to be there with us and will one day lead us home.

Naomi Starkey

This compilation copyright © BRF 2006
Authors retain copyright in their own work
Illustrations copyright © Jane Bottomley, Chris Daunt and Ian Mitchell 2006

Published by
The Bible Reading Fellowship
First Floor, Elsfield Hall
15–17 Elsfield Way, Oxford OX2 8FG
Websites: www.brf.org.uk and www.quietspaces.org.uk

ISBN-10: 1 84101 482 6
ISBN-13: 978 1 84101 482 1
First published 2006
10 9 8 7 6 5 4 3 2 1 0

Acknowledgments
Unless otherwise stated, scripture quotations are taken from The New Revised Standard Version of the Bible, Anglicized Edition, copyright © 1989, 1995 by the Division of Christian Education of the National Council of the Churches of Christ in the USA, and are used by permission. All rights reserved.

Scriptures quoted from the Good News Bible published by The Bible Societies/HarperCollins Publishers Ltd, UK © American Bible Society 1966, 1971, 1976, 1992, used with permission.

Scripture quotations taken from the Contemporary English Version of the Bible published by HarperCollins Publishers, copyright © 1991, 1992, 1995 American Bible Society.

Scripture quotations taken from the Holy Bible, New International Version, copyright © 1973, 1978, 1984 by International Bible Society, are used by permission of Hodder & Stoughton Limited. All rights reserved. 'NIV' is a registered trademark of International Bible Society. UK trademark number 1448790.

Scripture quotations from THE MESSAGE. Copyright © Eugene H. Peterson 1993, 1994, 1995. Used by permission of NavPress Publihing.

'Walking' by Anne Brown from Even Angels Tread Softly, a Mothers' Union anthology of poetry (ISBN 0 85943 064 2). The Mothers' Union, 24 Tufton Street, London SW1P 3RB. Tel: 0207 222 5533. Website: www.themothersunion.org

A catalogue record for this book is available from the British Library

Printed by Gutenberg Press, Tarxien, Malta

CONTENTS

Wilderness:

the place of testing

R. Alastair Campbell is a Baptist
minister who taught New Testament
at Spurgeon's College. He has
worked overseas in Nigeria and
Nepal and currently teaches at the
United Theological College of the West
Indies in Jamaica. BRF has published
his guide to the New Testament, 'The
Story We Live By' (2004).

Today, if we think about wilderness at all, it is likely to
be in a positive sense. Wilderness describes those areas
of the world that are unspoilt, untamed. In our shrinking
global village, we are painfully aware that such areas
are getting fewer and smaller. Wilderness is something
to be *preserved*. In the USA, wilderness is protected by
an Act of Congress, which defines it as follows: 'A
wilderness, in contrast to those areas where man and
his own works dominate the landscape, is hereby
recognized as an area where the earth and community
of life are untrammelled by man, where man himself is
a visitor who does not remain.' Notice the value
judgment implied by the word 'untrammelled'! Jaded

city-dwellers dream of being able to escape to the wilderness, at least for a holiday and with sufficient 'mod cons' to make life bearable!

The perspective of the biblical writers was rather different. The lands in which much of the Bible story unfolds have always been dry. Life tends to be concentrated in towns and cities where there are springs of water. Civilization is to be found along the great river valleys, the Nile in Egypt and the Euphrates in Babylon. Much of the area in between is, by contrast, 'wilderness', described as 'a marginal geographical area that does not provide sufficient resources to sustain long-term community existence'.[1] As such, wilderness is not so much something to be preserved as something to be preserved from.

Those who live in such areas have to move from place to place, like the patriarchs, Abraham, Isaac and Jacob, moving from one source of water to another as their flocks and herds consume the scanty supplies of grass. They live a nomadic existence on the margins of the flourishing civilization of the Canaanite towns where they are denied the right to settle, sustained by God's promise that he will bring them into a land of their own where the wilderness will be a thing of the past.

The biblical writers are glad to live in towns, and their perception of the wilderness is generally negative, as we can see from the language they use to describe it. We find the wilderness described as 'an arid wasteland with poisonous snakes and scorpions', as 'a howling wilderness waste' (Deuteronomy 8:15; 32:10), 'a parched land', 'the land of drought' (Hosea 2:3; 13:5), 'a land not sown', 'a land of deserts and pits… of drought and deep darkness', 'a land ruined and laid waste' (Jeremiah 2:2, 6; 9:12). The wilderness means desolation, aridity and death.

On the Day of Atonement the wilderness is seen as a fitting place to release the scapegoat that carries all the sins that have been confessed over it. The scapegoat is said to be sent 'to Azazel' (Leviticus 16:10), who may possibly be a demon. Certainly, in later Jewish and Christian tradition, the wilderness was

…he will bring them into a land of their own where the **wilderness will be a thing of the past**

Life in all its fullness is to be found in community, not in isolation; in the city, not the wilderness

...God will woo Israel and lead her back to the wilderness

thought of as the abode of demons. When God judges a nation, he allows it to become a wilderness. When he saves and restores, the wilderness is turned into a fertile place. For the psalmist, the wilderness is a symbol of spiritual dryness and of God's absence.

Often 'the wilderness' refers not just to a geographical reality but to a specific period of Israel's history, the 40 years that Israel spent between leaving Egypt and entering the promised land, and here the picture is more ambiguous. To be sure, this also can be seen as a negative time, a time of rebellion and punishment. Worshippers are reminded not to harden their hearts when God speaks to them, as the people did 'when your ancestors tested me, and put me to the proof, though they had seen my work' (Psalm 95:9). The exodus story records how Israel murmured against God because of the harsh conditions of the wilderness, and especially how they at first refused to enter the promised land because of the giants reported to be living there.

As a result, the wilderness became a place of judgment and discipline. God decrees, 'None of the people who have seen my glory and the signs that I did in Egypt and in the wilderness, and yet have tested me these ten times and have not obeyed my voice, shall see the land that I swore to give to their ancestors; none of those who despised me shall see it.' Instead, 'As for you, your dead bodies shall fall in this wilderness. And your children shall be shepherds in the wilderness for forty years, and shall suffer for your faithlessness, until the last of your dead bodies lies in the wilderness' (Numbers 14:22–23, 32–33). The wilderness period is remembered as one of testing, failure and judgment: 'They grumbled in their tents, and did not obey the voice of the Lord. Therefore he raised his hand and swore to them that he would make them fall in the wilderness' (Psalm 106:25–26).

The wilderness is also remembered as the time when Israel was forged into a nation. Deuteronomy in particular looks back over the wilderness period and reminds Israel of how good God has been to them. He chose them as his own possession. He sustained them and provided for them water from the rock, manna from heaven: 'The clothes on your back did not wear out and your feet did not swell these forty years' (Deuteronomy 8:4). God lived among them by means of the tent of meeting. He guided them by the pillar of fire and cloud and brought them safely to the place of opportunity in which they now stand, and if the living was far from easy, this is now seen as necessary discipline: 'Remember the long way that the Lord your God has led you these forty years in the wilderness, in order to humble you, testing you to know what was in your heart, whether or not you would keep his commandments... Know then in your heart that as a parent disciplines a child so the Lord your God disciplines you' (vv. 2, 5).

Jeremiah challenges his generation with the reminder of the wilderness as a time of honeymoon: 'Thus says the Lord: I remember the devotion of your youth, your love as a bride, how you followed me in the wilderness, in a land not sown' (Jeremiah 2:2). Most strikingly, Hosea, who has harsh words for Israel's repeated unfaithfulness, can envisage a time when God will woo Israel and lead her back to the wilderness and to the love and obedience that characterized that period: 'Therefore, I will now allure her, and bring her into the wilderness, and speak tenderly to her. From there I will give her her vineyards, and make the Valley of Achor a door of hope. There she shall respond as in the days of her youth, as at the time when she came out of the land of Egypt' (Hosea 2:14–15).

The wilderness is transitory and transitional, like the sufferings of this present life

The word of God comes to John the Baptist in the wilderness

In line with this, Isaiah can speak of the return from Babylon as a new exodus: 'A voice cries out: "In the wilderness prepare the way of the Lord, make straight in the desert a highway for our God"' (Isaiah 40:3). God will do a new thing that resembles yet surpasses the old thing: 'I will make a way in the wilderness and rivers in the desert' (43:19).

The New Testament has little to say about the wilderness. The story largely takes place in the towns of Galilee and in the cities of the Mediterranean. It is true, though, that in the Gospels significant things happen in the wilderness. The word of God comes to John the Baptist in the wilderness, and this is seen to fulfil Isaiah's prophecy just mentioned. Jesus is 'led by the Spirit in the wilderness, where for forty days he was tempted by the devil' (Luke 4:1–2). Later, he feeds the great crowd with bread and fish, and this, too, takes place in the desert.

The point of all these stories is to portray Jesus as the new Moses and greater than Moses, who brings about a new exodus for God's people and feeds them with the bread of God. John's preaching in the desert shows the coming of Jesus to be the coming of God. Jesus' temptations in the wilderness repeat Israel's wilderness experience, as the reference to Deuteronomy ('Man does not live on bread alone', Luke 4:4, NIV) makes plain, and they show him to be the fulfilment of Israel's hopes and longings. John's Gospel draws out at length the way in which the feeding miracle recalls Moses and the manna in the wilderness and surpasses it.

In none of these stories is the wilderness exemplary, as if to say that the wilderness is the place to go if you want to hear God's voice, or overcome temptation, or feed on the bread of life. The focus is on Jesus, showing him to be the Christ, though of course it is true that on occasion we read of Jesus seeking desert places for prayer and rest, and there is a possible lesson for us in that.

Paul, after his conversion, went to Arabia. It is possible that this was for a time of reflection and

> John's preaching in the desert shows the coming of Jesus to be the **coming of God**

reassessment, but if so, his choice of destination is more likely to have been because Arabia is the location of Sinai rather than because it is desert as such. Paul, like Elijah before him, was going back to the roots of his faith in response to his new experience of Christ.

It is in the book of Revelation that wilderness is given a positive symbolic meaning. The wilderness first appears as a place of refuge. In the allegory of chapter 12, the woman, who represents the people of God, flees from the dragon, or Satan, and finds refuge in the desert, recalling the way in which Israel escaped from Pharaoh and found sanctuary in the wilderness. In a later passage, the angelic interpreter carries John away into the desert so that he can see clearly the true nature of the Roman empire and its civilization. Like Egypt before her, Rome is magnificent and powerfully attractive, but her charms are those of a whore, enticing people with her idolatrous claims to give their allegiance to the state rather than to God. Only by coming out of her into the simplicity of the wilderness will you be able to see her for what she is. In the fourth century, many Christians turned their backs on what they saw as a comfortable and compromising church to seek God in the desert and do battle with its demons there.

Yet the book of Revelation does not end with an unspoilt wilderness but with a city, and in this it is true to the Bible's perspective on the wilderness as a whole. Wilderness may be necessary as a place of preparation, discipline and even judgment, but it is not the ultimate destination of God's people, either in the Old Testament or in the New. God's great new world is not a rural paradise but a shining city in which human achievement is celebrated, not obliterated; from which flows a river of life that will bring healing to the nations and make the wilderness a wilderness no more. The wilderness is transitory and transitional, like the sufferings of this present life. Suffering and death were necessary to effect our salvation, but we do not glory in them. God is on the side of life, not death, and life in all its fullness is to be found in community, not in isolation; in the city, not the wilderness. ■

NOTES

1 T.D. Alexander and D.W. Baker (eds.), *Dictionary of the Old Testament: Pentateuch* (IVP, 2004), p. 893.

Around the world, around the corner

Travels with the Mothers' Union across the globe

Most travel is by plane or boat, with the MU providing canoes

Fleur Dorrell is head of spirituality and prayer for the Mothers' Union and is an experienced retreat attender and leader.

The word 'wilderness' in different languages has overtones of wild desolation, and isolation. Yet, if we take a brief tour around some of the remote areas of the world where the Mothers' Union (MU) works, we shall see that even in the most isolated places, God can be at work through the efforts of ordinary people, bringing hope and healing into the lives of those around them.

Psalm 57:1

In you my soul takes refuge; in the shadow of your wings I will take refuge.

Our first stop is the Diocese of the Arctic, Canada, which covers four million square kilometres (a third of Canada). It stretches westwards from the border of Yukon Territory, and is bounded to the south by the 60th

We inhabit the spiritual desert of secularism and materialism

parallel. The east includes the north coast of Quebec from James Bay to the tip of Labrador. Counselling, hospital ministry and family studies provided by the MU are crucial, because there are high suicide rates among the Inuit, and increasing relationship breakdown. As the people number only 55,000, with Inuit living above the tree line and Indians living south, creating a better future for the children is vital for the Arctic's survival.

If we make a dramatic descent to the vast but sparsely populated Diocese of North West Australia, we find the MU Northern Outreach Fund. This facilitates the biennial clergy family and women's conferences, enabling the bishop's wife to travel to the remote parishes where the MU runs programmes assisting families, drug addicts, abused women and the Aboriginal community of Wiluna. Giving a Christian, supportive voice in these insular communities and especially to countless isolated women is invaluable.

Travelling north-east to Melanesia, where the MU is active in all eight

11

Women remain housebound, uneducated and powerless to change

> **The MU here is like a lighthouse to their self-worth and their potential future**

dioceses and where men can be 'associate members' only, we find over 14,000 members. Here, raising awareness of health issues such as TB, malaria, family planning, sexually transmitted diseases, and HIV/AIDS forms the MU's priority work, in contrast with the smaller but nonetheless important projects of bee-keeping and ice-cream making.

The Solomon Islands have been affected by ethnic conflict between Guadalcanal and Malaita Islands, although a new agreement was signed in October 2000. The church in Melanesia and the MU work hard at breaking down distrust, but transport and communication are a major problem as some of the islands have no roads; most travel is by plane or boat, with the MU providing canoes.

Banks and Torres Diocese stretches over 14 inhabited islands and is in the northern part of the Vanuatu archipelago in the southern Pacific Ocean. The MU sees leadership training and workshops on violence against women as paramount because one of the corollaries of isolation here is women's oppression. Given that 70 per cent of the world's illiterate are women, because boys have preferential access to education, this tragic cycle perpetuates itself in all the areas of the world where women remain housebound, uneducated and powerless to change.

Continuing west, 75 per cent of Papua New Guinea's main island is covered with tropical rainforests, rugged mountain peaks and high valleys, making access difficult. Unusually, however, it is in the more remote parts here that the men are the most collaborative— helping women to prepare meals on hot stones in the ground and cleaning their dwellings. Despite bitter hardships, the MU has over 20,000 members in the five dioceses of Aipo, Rongo, Dogura, Popondota and Port Moresby with the New Guinea Islands. It is involved in hospital and community outreach, HIV/AIDS and gender education (PNG has the highest rate of HIV/AIDS transmission in the Pacific), communication, and multifarious projects in fishing, cooking and handicrafts.

Luke 11:17

Jesus said to them, 'Every kingdom divided against itself becomes a desert, and house falls on house.'

The MU is central to 1.5 million African women. In Tanzania's Mount Kilimanjaro Diocese, they run Bible study groups and micro-projects such as house rentals, nut growing and nursery schools. In Morogoro Diocese—part semi-desert and part fertile farming land—MU pastoral activities include visiting the sick, disabled and bereaved. In the parishes, the members are involved in agricultural activities, sewing and tree planting. Through seminars and workshops, they also increase awareness of family responsibilities, environmental conservation, HIV and AIDS, and educate against the long-established cultural practice of female genital mutilation.

Leaving mainland east Africa, we arrive at Madagascar and Antananarivo in the Indian Ocean. The preservation of the *fihavanana* (having good relationships with all people) is very important culturally and underpins all the MU's activities, as do building up the spiritual welfare of families and upholding the Malagasy policy to alleviate poverty and eradicate illiteracy in the rural areas. Women are considered 'lower' than men, with no rights to education or decision-making in any aspect of their daily life. The MU here is like a lighthouse to their self-worth and their potential future.

Proverbs 30:5

Every word of God proves true; he is a shield to those who take refuge in him.

Returning to Africa, we find Kimberley and Kuruman Diocese in an arid, semi-desert region of southern Africa. Life is difficult and the weather harsh, with cold winters and scorching summers. Poverty is rife and most people are subsistence farmers or miners. MU members teach craft work and organize rural self-help and outreach programmes. They offer workshops on family issues and, pertinently for such

Even in the most isolated places, God can be at work

13

Our perceived freedom and independence have enslaved us

an isolated region, on listening to God and listening to others.

El Obeid Diocese in Sudan comprises six states: North, South and West Kordofan and North, South and West Darfur. The long-running civil war has split the diocese into two; part of the southern area cannot be reached from El Obeid. This is one of the most arid settlements in Sudan, lying in the western desert. Despite the war and its continued atrocities, the MU is active in teaching and visiting hospital patients and prisoners, and assisting both Christian and Muslim refugees.

In south-west Uganda lies Kinkizi Diocese, bordering the Democratic Republic of Congo on the western side and with one-quarter in the Great Rift Valley. The rest of the area is mountainous with deep valleys, criss-crossed by a number of rivers. Workshops on reproductive health for

adolescents, peace building and human rights, leadership and management skills provide the substance of MU mission here, as well as financial support for schoolgirls who are unable to afford education.

Psalm 121:1-2

I lift up my eyes to the hills—from where will my help come? My help comes from the Lord, who made heaven and earth.

Finally, we approach western Europe. Geographically, Kilmocomogue in West Cork, Ireland, is the most south-westerly and remote branch in the MU. They have only 26 members but as a branch they are particularly concerned with CoAction, a local organization looking after the needs of the physically and intellectually challenged. Most summers, they provide a barbecue for Chernobyl children (and their host families) on holiday in the area.

When Gandhi was asked what he thought about western civilisation, he said that it would be a good idea! 'Wilderness' in the west is much greater than the diverse areas mentioned above, because we inhabit the spiritual desert of secularism and materialism; we experience a famine of the soul in an unparalleled wilderness of loneliness, depression and unhappiness. We are so rich in material terms: the growth in food, money, communication, technology and travel serves to accommodate our obsession with choice. We have a wealth beyond comprehension to the 1.3 billion people who live on less than a dollar a day, yet we are more infertile, over-stressed, unfulfilled and trapped than ever. There is so much noise now that silence is considered frightening.

Our perceived freedom and independence have enslaved us. We think we do not need God because our materialistic props prevent us from facing our inner selves. Our communication has become more virtual as we email or text our most private thoughts rather than daring to talk in person. We fear and deny the realities of ageing and death. And we are bewildered! We can't even go to a supermarket without having to decide between 18 different breakfast cereals, while 30,000 children die daily.

We need to seek a balanced and peace-filled lifestyle that will provide fertile ground for spiritual enrichment and self-growth. We need to find places where we can be alone with God, so that he can refine and nourish us. MU members in remote corners of the world are often more in touch with God, more community-minded, with a stronger and more powerful spirit of fellowship than we could imagine, because their priorities are radically different. Although they may live far apart, they support and pray for each other and are truer friends than the neighbours we never speak to on our own doorsteps.

The MU Wave of Prayer is our system for praying for each other and our dioceses worldwide: it transcends the barriers of geography and time as it is said daily at midday. This is a great model for discipleship because by praying for each other we are challenged to think beyond our own needs. What we say, buy, believe in, work for and eat, and how we spend our leisure time, all affect people around the world. If, for instance, you have drunk tea or coffee, eaten bananas, chocolate or nuts, or worn cotton in the last 24 hours, you will have taken part in a massive trade war between the developed and developing worlds.

Why not spend time reflecting on your neighbours' and community's

We need to seek a balanced and peace-filled lifestyle

needs and how you would prioritize them? What could you do to make a small difference on your doorstep? And consider reaching out in prayer to those working in the literal wilderness places in the world, that they may sense God with them, sustaining and encouraging them in all they do. ■

Can YOU hear the singing?

Pamela Evans enjoys encouraging others in their discipleship through writing, speaking and spiritual direction. Her books, 'Driven Beyond the Call of God' and 'Building the Body', are published by BRF.

In my youth, I very much enjoyed being part of a parish church choir. One day, when a few minutes remained at the end of choir practice, one of the ancient members (I was a teenager; they must have been at least 40 years old) suggested finishing with 'The Wilderness'. This anthem by Sir John Goss takes its words from Isaiah 35. The choir had learned it before I joined, but I had no problem understanding their enthusiasm. As sopranos, altos, tenors and basses sang overlapping parts proclaiming 'streams in the desert' and telling of 'songs of everlasting joy', the exuberance was palpable.

Fast-forwarding more than 35 years... I'd become aware of what I can only describe as an area of desolation in the deepest part of my heart. Now and then it would remind me of its existence, but most of the time it was silent and frustratingly inaccessible to my attempts to get a handle on it. I didn't understand what had brought it into being, but I did know that I wanted to be free of it. I and others had prayed for healing, and I'd seen much benefit as a result, but an area of 'desert' remained.

One day, as I was travelling to meet a friend for further prayer, I felt God saying, 'Today's the day.' And it was!

After the Lord had been at work in profound ways that defy description, I began to 'hear' joyful singing—about waters breaking out in the wilderness and streams in the desert; about the ransomed of the Lord singing songs of joy. And my heart sang, too! The words of the anthem, not sung for half a lifetime, had come bursting out. They provided much-needed assurance that God had indeed brought healing and restoration.

Remembering

Shortly before his crucifixion, Jesus told his disciples that the Holy Spirit would remind them of everything he'd said (John 14:26). Given the traumatic time ahead, it's just as well they had expert help with remembering his instructions! But this experience of the Holy Spirit jogging the memory is one for which followers of Jesus continue to be thankful today.

'I have hidden your word in my heart that I might not sin against you,' says the psalmist (Psalm 119:11, NIV). As a young Christian I was urged to memorize key verses, and did my best. It's probably true, though, that singing implanted most of what my brain has retained. By God's grace, psalms and canticles chanted in my teens often pop up at just the right time, when I'm mulling over something for work or when praying. They're a rich resource, as are more recent worship songs based on scripture.

If you're aware that there's very little of the Bible in your memory—you've only recently become a Christian, or you

> Stay with the picture, and listen to anything God might be wanting to say through it

struggle with learning anything by heart—don't fret. Start now! Many people find songs and hymns based on scripture a good place to begin, but try asking the Creator who made you what will work best for you. The key point is to cooperate with God by filling your mind with things the Holy Spirit might conceivably wish to bring to your remembrance.

Picturing

My prayer partner tells me that she struggles to memorize words, yet has no difficulty with picturing scenes. Her experience, and the encouraging ending to the time of prayer I've described, point to ways in which imagination may be used to serve

God's purposes. It's worth noting that while, in our culture, imagination is often linked to unreality and fantasy—some of it unutterably vile—God intended 'the eyes of our hearts' to be

Singing

implanted most of what my brain has retained

God

intended 'the eyes of our hearts' to be conduits for the truth

conduits for the truth and treasures of heaven. The apostle Paul understood this. Writing to the Ephesians, he said, 'I pray… that the eyes of your heart may be enlightened in order that you may know the hope to which [God] has called you, the riches of his glorious inheritance in the saints, and his incomparably great power for us who believe' (Ephesians 1:18–19, NIV).

In today's world we're bombarded with images that can so easily pollute this picture-making capacity of our minds. If you're aware that your imagination has been contaminated by being misused, it would be wise to pray first (or ask others to pray with you) for cleansing. If the idea of using your imagination as you read scripture is new, you may feel uneasy. It's good to pray a

prayer for protection, asking God to come by his Holy Spirit and set a guard around you, especially your mind and heart. Then, check out any pictures and thoughts that come, and see if they're in tune with scripture. You may find it helpful to make notes in a journal.

Isaiah 35 could be a good place to start. Read it through very slowly, a phrase at a time. Can you 'see' the parched land of the desert, cracked and with no sign of life? (Don't rush on—stay with the picture, and listen to anything God might be wanting to say through it.) Now 'watch' as a trickle of water arrives, gradually becoming a stream, and then a gushing torrent. What happens to the burning sand? Can you see the flowers springing up? What is God saying as you contemplate this picture of regeneration and renewal?

How about verses 3 and 4: are you able to visualize the weak and dispirited people? What is their body language conveying? Weariness? Fear? Despair? What happens as they hear these words of hope?

Energize the limp hands, strengthen the rubbery knees. Tell fearful souls, 'Courage! Take heart! God is here, right here, on his way to put things right and redress all wrongs.

He's on his way! He'll save you!' (THE MESSAGE)

Picture the faces of blind men, women and children as they begin to see—and those with all sorts of physical disabilities, now able to do things they believed impossible (vv. 5–6).

God has the power to deliver on his promises—and he's on his way! Isaiah 35 is one of the passages we may use to keep our hearts expectant during the waiting time.

If your life has much in common with the wilderness, ask God to help you lift your eyes from the dust to what lies beyond. Can you picture that highway (vv. 8–10), bringing a sense of direction to the featureless wasteland? Purged of all evil and danger, it's for those who have been redeemed and ransomed. Can you see them journeying together... sense the atmosphere, rich with celebration, as they arrive in the holy city? Can you hear the singing?

Whether or not you find it easy to visualize the scene and 'hear' the joyful voices, if you've trusted in Christ this glad homecoming is your destiny, too. And that highlights an important function of picturing—our imaginations helping our hearts to embrace biblical truths that our minds already know, helping us to enter fully into aspects of reality that otherwise we might only glimpse from afar. Note the important distinction from fantasizing: this exercise is reality-based imagining, rooted in biblical truth.

Enlarging our vision

In the days and weeks that followed the healing of my mini-desert, I thanked God for what he'd done. As I did so, I was able to 'see' a swathe of crocuses (35:1)—probably more English country garden than Middle Eastern desert, but truly a 'symphony of song and colour' (v. 2, *THE MESSAGE*). Some months later, while I was thanking God for what he'd done in my life, it was as if I turned a corner. I realized that the swathe of crocuses I'd seen before was only a tiny part of a wide valley carpeted with blooms. Wow! As yet, I don't know the significance of this extended picture. What I do know is that God is in the business of restoration, redemption and healing; of offering a safe way through the wilderness in the company of others on the same journey. I sense that he's wanting to enlarge my vision of what he can do—and perhaps your vision, too. ∎

God is in the business of **restoration, redemption** and **healing**

Writing for the SOUL

What do John Donne, Louisa May Alcott, Dame Cicely Saunders and C.S. Lewis have in common? They were all at various times journal keepers, recording their days in writing—primarily for their own reflection.

The journals and memoirs of the famous, funny or influential are interesting for the events they document and the character they reveal. Journalling for a Christian plays a different role. It will still portray our life story, but the practice of keeping a journal of faith as well as of life means that we share that story with God.

So what does journalling our faith mean in practical terms? First, there is a hazy distinction to be made between journalling and keeping a diary. A diary is primarily a record of events. It may become a journal over time, just as a journal may reduce its vision and purpose to that of a diary. But a diary often remains a record of what we have done in our life and where, when and how we have done it.

A journal, on the other hand, records our response to that life and reflects on its myriad details. We lay out our days on the page, put our heart on the lines, and as we write, we learn more about ourselves, our life, and the God whom we recognize as being intimately involved in it. In doing so, we offer that life and reflection to God for his response. Direction and wisdom often come out of that experience, offering a new dimension to our relationship with him.

The process of writing my journal clears away

Wendy Bray is a freelance writer and columnist for a regional daily paper. She is fascinated by personal stories of faith and by the way in which journalling makes us aware of being part of God's 'story'. Wendy has also written 'In the Palm of God's Hand' and 'The Art of Waiting' for BRF.

God
is joyfully
involved in
every activity

distractions and helps me to focus on what really matters. It clarifies the meaning of my response to events, helping me discover things I didn't realize about myself and to recognize the value of my relationships. Most importantly, it gives a context into which God can speak.

Journalling helps me to recognize what I call a 'theology of experience': the way in which God is joyfully involved in every activity, detail, decision, hesitation and catch of breath in my daily life.

> **Many of us see our experience more clearly in terms of pictures**

That recognition was never more evident than in the journals I kept throughout my diagnosis and treatment of cancer. They were not originally written for others to read, but were eventually shared through publication (*In the Palm of God's Hand*, BRF, 2002)

Those journals were the basis of a very real dialogue in prayer. It was a dialogue that not only covered the spiritual questions, the fears, doubt and hope in that whole experience, but also the practical concerns and the funny asides. There was no audible voice or heated heavenly debate, but a traceable father-and-daughter conversation that mirrored all that was going on in my life. Looking back on it now, nearly seven years later, I am still amazed by the joy and intimacy it contains.

So how do we keep a faith journal that reflects every element of our Christian lives? My answer to that question is always the same: just begin.

There are few rules about journal keeping, although I think there are two essentials: write often and write honestly. But when things are bad, don't let your honesty bury you in misery. Rather, let God read what you have written and lift you out of it!

In practical terms, all that's needed is time, space, paper and pen. An expensive notebook isn't necessary, although it helps to be able to keep notes in order. Most supermarkets sell spiral-bound exercise books that are easy to write in and hardy enough for the frequent bending and page turning that practical journal keeping requires. Neither does a journal have

We lay out our days on the page, put our heart on the lines

to be added to every day, or written in the same way each time, although regularity builds a rhythm and commitment to the purpose. Remember, a journal is there to serve us, not for us to become a slave to it.

I choose to write my journal at the same time as I pray or read my Bible, at the beginning and the end of the day. It's an arrangement that suits me well, but time and place are personal choices. Sometimes there just won't be anything we want to write. On other days we will write long into the night—not because we 'did' so much in the day, but because we felt so much, observed so much, learnt so much, and want to capture it. I have sometimes written several pages in reflection on one conversation, and just a line or two on a special event.

The journalling process begins before and goes on long after we have opened and closed our books or papers, because whenever we journal we will follow a routine of 'R's:

First we *recall*—not every moment of the day, but those incidents, words, responses and feelings that have been significant. The conversations we learnt from, the encounters that delighted us, the words we read or heard spoken or sung, the sad things that challenged us, the funny things that reminded us of the need to laugh often; anything—which is *everything* that God may speak through.

Then we *write*—in our own words, about our experience as it is remembered and for as long as we wish. There's no need to worry about grammar, handwriting or spelling, because (usually) no one but ourselves will read our words. Often, the less considered we are as we write, the more honest our words and the more immediate our emotion. We can get lost in feeling, find metaphors for emotion and connect our words to our experience with spontaneity. We may even ask ourselves questions or note down queries to follow up or actions to take.

Then we will *respond*. I stop and pray at this point, asking God to show me what I need to recognize in my own words: a resentment or critical attitude, a preoccupation with myself or neglect of another. I read

No need to worry about grammar, handwriting or spelling

There was no audible voice or heated heavenly debate, but a traceable **father-and-daughter conversation** that mirrored all that was going on in my life

Direction and wisdom often come out of that experience

through my journal entry and respond to what my own words tell me about what is happening not just in my life, but also in my heart and mind.

I give myself a few moments to *reflect* on what God may have been whispering through those lines. It's at this point that I often add the most useful part of my journal entry: a *reminder*. It could be a sharp observation or a sad conclusion about my own need to change, a reassurance of God's encouragement, or a memo of his word clearly spoken by a friend. These are often 'penny dropping' moments.

Weeks later, I will *remember* something that I wrote and find that it connects to my present experience. I will pick out patterns in my writing, reading and praying that God has been weaving through my life, and through the pages of my journal. These patterns illustrate the way in which he has reassured, reminded, guided, even disciplined me as I have written.

That's when I will take time to *review* my journal, looking back on that pattern and process. I may even discern some principles for *redirection* of my life. When I first reviewed the journals that made up *In the Palm of God's Hand*, I noticed an astounding pattern of question and answer, doubt and reassurance, which both encouraged and honoured my attempts.

When I invite others to keep journals, they often reply, 'I can't write.' But journalling is not just for writers. Many of us see our experience more clearly in terms of pictures. That may help us to use metaphor in writing, but may also make it easier for us to draw or paint a journal. One of my close friends is an accomplished artist. Her journals are sketchbooks full of the most beautiful drawings combined with words and phrases. They equally express a special dialogue with a God who finds more than one way to communicate. Interestingly, that very process has encouraged her to write with more confidence.

The journalling experience simply asks us to express our life on paper and reflect upon it in the company of God. It's an invitation that we would do well to accept: it might just be life-changing. ■

The desert

of mind-sickness

Jenny Robertson is a writer whose books for children and adults have been widely transated. She has written 'Strength of the Hills' for BRF. After a number of years spent working in Russia, Poland and Spain, she is now based in her native Scotland.

My wilderness experience began 15 years ago when a consultant psychiatrist interviewed my husband and me in a bare room in a mental hospital. The walls were covered with some sort of job-lot paint, devoid of any decoration. The prognosis he gave us was stark as well.

'Your daughter is very unwell and may never live a normal life.'

That was all. He probably said something about 'a schizophrenic-type illness', but we were too shocked to take anything else in, although it is well recognized that bad news needs time to digest and space to ask more questions. It's also known that close family and friends are directly affected by a relative's mental illness, but no support was offered, no further explanation given. Everything I now know about schizophrenia and psychotic illness, I have found out for myself.

Although, with every illness, it is

25

There is no beauty in the desert called pain

Severe mental illness
kills not life, but function

recognized that a speedy diagnosis and speedy treatment mean a better outcome, we spent years of anguish before we were finally able to admit our desperately ill 20-year-old daughter into mental hospital. Even then, despite court orders, she was no sooner admitted than she ran away.

'It's so complex,' a psychiatrist justified this slowness. 'There's no predictive test. We need to go slowly and carefully. There are never enough funds, and it's such a horrendous diagnosis to give a young person. There's so much stigma attached to mental illness.'

Battering against unyielding doors, I received a letter from my daughter's doctor, which said, 'I always find it difficult when a relative of someone I see professionally tries to be more helpful than the person themselves would wish. But thank you for your interest in the widest possible sense.'

We had plunged into a wilderness without any reprieve this side of eternity.

The desert is a bleak place, devoid of comfort, scorching the skin, drying all natural juices. Night brings no respite. The temperature drops and the cold pierces to the marrow of the bones. The searing day-time heat and dryness of the desert exhaust our resources. Defence mechanisms that usually protect us cannot withstand the pitiless heat of the desert. The props we thought were faith are stripped away.

The desert strips us of all appearance of respectability, even of self-respect. And this is especially true when we enter the wilderness of mind-sickness and scale the awesome mountains of the mind: those 'cliffs of fall / Frightful, sheer, no-man-fathomed', as a sufferer from severe depression, the priest-poet Gerard Manley Hopkins, put it.

My daughter has been wounded on the jagged peaks of psychosis for over 17 years—half her life. This gentle young woman has been taken into psychiatric hospital by the police, held down and forcibly injected. Back at home with her husband, she sat beside the empty space where her baby's cot once stood, knowing she had lost the right to be a mother to the daughter she loves.

She wrote to me once from mental hospital, after her daughter had been adopted by family friends: 'Who will deliver me from this darkness? Who will respect a married wife for her potential as mother to her children?

'How I long to play on the sands where little ones go with their mummies and daddies to be free, far from criminals and prisons, ransacking and injustice. I love to see the snow fall softly across streets and houses and towns where the only sound is the noise of muffled cars. The mind has many mountains. Sometimes it is respected, but often I feel it is being completely destroyed.'

'There is nothing benign in psychosis,' a doctor once truly said.

Friends at church tell me how hard they find it. 'I don't know what to say to her. She comes out with such strange things,' one person complained. 'I find it easier to cope with Johnny with learning difficulties,' another told me honestly. 'Have you been cursed, involved in the occult, had an abortion?' other well-meaning people of prayer have asked my husband and me. And a Christian counsellor, sent to see us by no less a person than our bishop, said, 'You are a sick family and your daughter is bearing your symptoms.'

My daughter still sees her husband, but he couldn't cope with her difficulties. She lives in supported accommodation now. She spent over three years in mental hospital waiting for this place. I visited her in the long-stay ward on the eve of her 30th birthday. We sat in the hospital grounds. I tried to draw comfort from the trees and well-kept lawns around

The props we thought were faith are stripped away

us, while she voiced her frustration. 'Mum, when will I get out of here? You don't understand the pain I'm in. I'm depressed to the point of death. Three whole years! I have interviews, phone calls. No one comes up with anything. I want to have more babies. I want to have a home. Please help me, Mum. It's horrible in here. The medication makes me ill, but they don't care. They drug

Jesus... comes through locked doors on wounded feet

A wilderness without any reprieve

you to the eyeballs but they won't let you sleep. They barge into my room and yell, "Get up!" I've been through so much, I can barely manage to be. Mum, do something about it. Mum, help me.'

She dropped her cigarette end among a litter of others beneath the trees and sucked her thumb.

Severe mental illness kills not life, but function. The commonplace things of everyday life prove impossible: getting up to face a new day, personal hygiene, even making a cup of coffee all become hugely difficult. I have seen improvements in what is called 'care in the community' over the last terrible years, but when the afflicted person concerned has no insight into her needs, she cannot take advantage of available

support. So areas of hope open up, only to be closed to us as yet another possible shelter in the wilderness crumbles before the unremitting ravages of mind-sickness.

In the desert, tested by the Evil One, Jesus refused to act against the laws of nature and use God's power for his own ends. Accused later of being deluded, he was never under any illusions.

We find it hard to face any kind of pain—and we are right not to underestimate its horror. The wilderness of pain puts each sufferer into the category the rest of us label 'unfortunate'. It raises barriers between us. We can guess at, but never feel another's pain. Pain is therefore entirely individual. Its arid landscape isolates and dispossesses the person, even of words. Pain becomes a kind of universal Esperanto comprehended only by those who have been rendered dumb.

There is no beauty in the desert called pain, and there seems to be no God. The level of separation seems too high. God is good. How can a good God send pain? Pain alienates, so how can there be pain in God? And if there is pain in God, why should I seek God at all? I desire beauty, colour, warmth, comfort, sufficient food and drink, not the harsh, hurtful contours of the wilderness of pain.

So, desperately in need of a solution, I turn back to Jesus—and I see the vulnerability he accepted for me. Refusing Satan's easy solutions, Jesus chooses the wilderness and learns to accept the cross. It is only when this part of the Gospel becomes our inner experience that we learn the folly of easy judgments. The dark place of dereliction and seeming rejection reveals Jesus who comes through locked doors on wounded feet. He blesses his fearful friends with hands that have been deeply scarred.

The Bible shows us that the whole universe is involved in the salvation of God. Paul expresses hope that 'glorious freedom' will liberate all creation (Romans 8:21). In the desert, tested by Satan, comforted by angels, Jesus discovered the dance of creation. The great promises of the prophets were realized: 'I will give you treasures hidden in dark and secret places. Then you will know that I, the Lord God of Israel, have called you by name' (Isaiah 45:3, CEV).

Jesus found that the desert was charged with the love of God. My daughter loves God. Sometimes she asks, 'Why has God done this to me?' The other day she prayed, 'Lord, you know I love you. Thank you for the family who care for my child. Please draw close to her and sing soft songs to her.'

My heart broke when I heard this prayer.

In the wilderness, stripped of every pretence, we learn compassion in which others feel not judged, but loved. ■

Walking

Why did we do it?
there we were
minding our own business
mending the nets
hoping for a better catch tomorrow.

And there he was
Walking
Talking of fishing a different kind
of fish
A crackpot
too long in the sun.

So, why am I here
and the others
following a man who is more than a
man?
And why do I feel
with a lifting in my inner being
that I am not walking away
  but
    towards…

ANNE BROWN

Music for the Soul:

O, for the wings of a dove!

Gordon Giles is vicar of St Mary Magdalene's Church, Enfield, north London. He contributes to BRF's 'New Daylight' notes and has also written 'The Music of Praise' (2002), 'The Harmony of Heaven' (2003) and 'O Come, Emmanuel' (2005) for BRF.

In 1927, a 15-year-old chorister called Ernest Lough made a recording of Felix Mendelssohn's lovely anthem 'Hear my Prayer', which contains the popular and famous section 'O, for the wings of a dove'. Lough, who died in 2000, was a chorister at the Temple Church in London, and the recording sold more than 300,000 copies in the first six months after its release—so many that the original master wore out, and it had to be recorded again within the year. It went on to become the first classical record to sell a million copies.

Consequently, Mendelssohn's eleven-minute anthem, or at least the second section, 'O, for the wings of a dove', must be one of the most well-known choral pieces. It begins with a treble (soprano) solo, presenting the opening words from Psalm 55, in which the psalmist pleads with God to be heard. Then the choir enter, emphasizing the expression of fear at the enemy's strength. The music is never inharmonious, but there is a sense of bewilderment before a pause is reached ('O God, hear my cry'). It is

Hear my prayer, O God, incline thy ear!
Thyself from my petition do not hide!
Take heed to me!
Hear how in prayer I mourn to thee!
Without thee all is dark, I have no guide.

The enemy shouteth, the godless come fast!
Iniquity, hatred, upon me they cast!
The wicked oppress me, ah, where shall I fly?
Perplexed and bewildered, O God, hear my cry!

My heart is sorely pained within my breast,
My soul with deathly terror is oppressed,
Trembling and fearfulness upon me fall.
With horror o'erwhelmed, Lord, hear me call!

O, for the wings, for the wings of a dove!
Far away, far away would I rove!
In the wilderness, build me a nest
And remain there for ever at rest.

WORDS BASED ON PSALM 55: W. BARTHOLOMEW
MUSIC: FELIX MENDELSSOHN-BARTHOLDY

as though the singer realizes that even in the face of danger, it is best to take a deep breath and remember that God is ever present. A stillness descends as he sings of his anguish and terror of death. But it is short-lived, and soon he cries out, 'Lord, hear me call!' The choir echo his outburst, apparently restoring the calm, and the music seems to ebb away, closing as much with resignation as with request.

But we are only halfway through the piece, and the ambiguity between panic and acceptance that has characterized the first half gives way to a vision of eternal rescue. In a beautiful reverie, the soloist sings 'O, for the wings of a dove'. Surprisingly perhaps, the wilderness becomes a refuge—the safe destination for a dove's flight. Sometimes the wilderness is a frightening place of loneliness, danger, hunger or extremes of temperature. But the psalmist characterizes it as a place of solitude and escape, of safety and peace, and it is significant that it is on a dove's wings that he is carried there.

The connection between doves and peace derives from the story of Noah, in which, after the flood waters have receded, a dove is sent out. She returns with an olive branch, indicating that God's judgment has passed and that restoration and forgiveness are now possible. Later, doves were associated with purity, as they could be sacrificed to God. In the New Testament, the Holy Spirit descends on Jesus at his baptism in the form of a dove. In art, the dove is sometimes shown as hovering over water, reminding us of the Spirit-baptism of Christ, and also of God's Spirit hovering over the waters at creation.

Ironically, in Psalm 55, the dove heads for the wilderness, but we might expect the wilderness to be devoid of

The psalmist flees his enemies for the solitude of the wilderness

water. After his baptism, Jesus is driven out into the wilderness, and it might seem that a wilderness is a place without God. The psalmist has a similar thought: out there in the wilderness, no one can get at you. Yet there is a difference between the wildernesses of the New Testament and of the Psalms. The psalmist flees his enemies for the solitude of the wilderness, whereas Jesus departs from human company to meet his enemy (Satan) in the desert wilderness. In both cases the enemy is vanquished.

Many of us are familiar with loneliness, and also with solitude. The two are different, although the physical realities of both may be identical. Emotionally, it is possible to feel lonely in a crowd, and to feel content while alone. These can be spiritual responses, too, and the key must surely lie in our attitude towards the silence and singularity of aloneness. In a world where radios and televisions can be companions for the lonely, it can be hard to be—or allow ourselves to be—truly alone. For some, the prospect can be an overwhelming terror, incorporating the fear that we and our world are isolated in a cosmological wilderness.

As Christians we do not believe this, so for us the silence of wilderness can be a place of encounter with our inner selves and with God. Oh, that in this busy world, our airwaves would resound with the flight of doves, bearing our souls to such a place, not of loneliness, but of solitude; not of fear, but of peace! ∎

Readings for reflection
Psalm 55
Mark 1:1–13

Music to listen to
Mendelssohn: *Hear my prayer* (containing 'O, for the wings of a dove'). There are many recordings, but Ernest Lough's is available cheaply on Naxos Nostalgia, serial no. 8120832. More modern recordings include *Agnus Dei: Music of Inner Harmony*, New College, Oxford, on Erato, serial no. 0630146342.

PRAYER

Christ our God, in the midst of the clamour of worldly conversation, bear us away on the wings of your Spirit to that place where there is no music, or silence, but one equal eternity. Amen.

Reading
in the wilderness

What do you read in the wilderness? What do you read if you find yourself in a place of testing and trial, of wandering? If where you are right now is a hostile place, barren, lonely...? Here are some suggestions— what I consider to be the most thought-provoking and stimulating recent 'wilderness stories'.

 My Heart will Choose to Say: a story of cancer, faith and growing up

John Musgrave (Authentic Media, 2005)

At the age of 30, John Musgrave was diagnosed with cancer and given a 20 per cent chance of survival. Three years later, John is still with us. This is the story of what happened, not only to John's body, but also to his heart. It is a book that is very much about the Lord, his mercy, and his church:

I managed to pull myself together but lost it when trying to join the congregation singing 'How great Thou art'. I couldn't get the words out and something totally broke inside me. I couldn't feel God close to me... I have never cried or been as hurt as I was at that moment. I literally wanted to curl up in a ball on the floor. I didn't understand where these emotions were coming from but could not calm myself down. Andy pushed his way down the aisle behind me and threw

Stephanie Heald has been responsible for developing Spring Harvest's literary event 'A Good Read', as well as the Spring Harvest publishing divison. She has spoken on workplace issues for the London Institute for Contemporary Christianity and also helped to run a local reading group.

his arms over my shoulders and held me. It felt like I was being held together, that without his arms I would crumble to the floor.

This is a moving and immensely encouraging story about how the church can act as a family. It is also an amazing story about an unpredictable but powerful God. Having said that, because it is story, it is not a theology. It doesn't explain the theory or resolve questions that you may have about healing.

The Shaming of the Strong:
the challenge of an unborn life

Sarah Williams (Kingsway, 2005)

⌐ ...awed
by the
faithfulness
of God

When Paul and Sarah Williams prayed for another child, they didn't expect the gift that the Lord was about to give them. At her 20-week scan, Sarah was told that the child would not survive birth as the child's chest was too small. The story that unfolds is powerful and humbling. It tells of God reaching down into a very dark place, of a mother going through the worst days of her life, almost dying herself, and then, two days later, delivering a child, Cerian, up to death, unto the Lord.

It gave me an insight into what it meant for God himself to send his Son for us

'I simply don't know how to do this, Lord,' I prayed. 'Every contraction is taking Cerian further from me and every inch of my body is resisting labour. I can't do it, I can't do it. Just let me out. I can't go through with this.' But I knew there was no way out... I knew I had to release her to [God]. It was as though I had to hand her over the walls of a besieged city in the thick of battle so that she could escape unharmed with him. The urgency of the picture galvanised me. Now I knew my role, I had to rise up with discipline and maturity like one who is trained for battle.

This book left me deeply moved, awed by the faithfulness of God, and by the knowledge of how very strong and sure is the faith that we have. It gave me an insight into the depth of pain and suffering that many people face, and left me shaking my head at their courage and witness. It helped me to see how God does use suffering, hugely, for good: as a witness to others, but much more than that, to draw us closer to him. It gave me an insight into what it meant for God himself to send his Son for us.

 ## Out of the Storm: questions and consolations from the book of Job

Christopher Ash (IVP, 2004)

This is a beautifully written background to the book of Job. The author writes:

Every Pastor knows that behind most front doors lies pain, often hidden, sometimes long-drawn-out, sometimes very deep. I was discussing how to preach a passage from Job with four fellow ministers, when I looked around the others. For a moment I lost my concentration when I realized that one of them, some years before, had lost his wife in a car accident in their first year of marriage. The second was bringing up a seriously handicapped daughter. The third had broken his neck and come within 2 mm of total paralysis or death six years previously. And the fourth had undergone repeated radical surgery, which had changed his life. As my concentration returned to Job, I thought, 'This book is not merely academic: it is both about and for people who know suffering.'

In this book a brilliant Bible teacher explains the text simply, deeply, poetically, asking 'wheelchair' questions, not remote, theoretical 'armchair' questions about suffering. It's not a book to skim through, but would work well as a devotional. ■

If you choose to read any of these books in a reading group or in your home group, here are some questions that you could use to frame your discussion.

❖ What does this book tell us about fear? About healing? About rejection?

❖ What does this book tell us about our role as a church, family or friends of those who are suffering? Try to think of a time when you have acted insensitively or 'put your foot in it' with someone who is suffering. What can we do, practically and spiritually, to help those we love who are suffering?

❖ How does this book proclaim God's goodness? Can a book on pain be encouraging?

❖ What is the difference between a theoretical response, a theological response and a 'wheelchair response' to suffering? Can you give examples?

❖ What, if anything, do we gain from suffering? What, if anything, do we learn from the suffering of others?

Looking after Number One

The Revd Dr Steve Griffiths is an ordained minister in the Church of England. He is currently Regional Centre Director, Centre for Youth Ministry, Cambridge. This abridged extract from his book 'God of the Valley' (BRF, 2003), describes his wilderness journey of bereavement.

> **Elijah got up, ate and drank, and the food gave him enough strength to walk forty days to Sinai, the holy mountain.**
>
> 1 KINGS 19:8

I was on a roll. I had never felt so good. I had been pursuing a concentrated training programme for the London Marathon for two months and was beginning to push myself beyond limits that I had previously only dreamt about. This particular afternoon, I had run for 13 miles and was feeling like I could go on for ever… Then disaster struck. My right leg gave way beneath me as my shin began to throb with pain. I collapsed in agony by the side of the road and rested there for a while… That afternoon marked the end of my Marathon hopes: I had shin splints and could not run on tarmac without causing the problem again. I was upset, of course, but still had other activities to keep me fit. I was swimming four miles a week and going to the gym three times a week...

Keeping fit had become very important to me. Perhaps there was a subconscious element about needing to control something. Clare was recovering well from her first bout of brain surgery but life was still extremely difficult for us both. I was looking after her during the day and, at night, she was having regular epileptic fits. Rebekah was less than a year old and I was carrying a great deal of the weight of parenthood. I had begun a new ministry and was studying for a PhD at the same time. While I gave the outward impression of coping well, emotionally I was sinking fast. I was tired, confused, disorientated, overworked and overstressed. I needed some release, both physically and emotionally, and my fitness routine was proving a good way of bringing some order into my life.

During the early years of Clare's remission, I managed to stay reasonably fit. After a while, however, it became impossible to continue my routine. Clare's epilepsy became less predictable and I was increasingly concerned that she would have a fit while I was out. Her right side became weaker as time went by and she was less able to undertake basic tasks such as opening cans, holding a kettle, getting in and out of the bath...

Gradually, I began to put on weight... I was working increasingly long hours and was becoming more tired and stressed. I was a smoker in those days, too, and was feeling increasingly ill with chest pains. I developed a bad skin condition on my hands that caused no small social embarrassment for me. In the year prior to Clare's death, her condition

---

While I gave the outward impression of coping well, emotionally **I was sinking fast**

---

deteriorated considerably and I found it almost impossible to leave her for any length of time on her own. Carrying almost all the burden of running a home, caring for a sick wife, bringing up a young daughter as well as working full time took an increasingly heavy toll on my health. I was absolutely exhausted, both physically and mentally. Due to time and energy constraints, it was often easier to rely on takeaways rather than cooking a healthy meal.

I was three-and-a-half stone overweight when Clare died. My skin condition was so bad that I often had my hands bandaged. The levels of stress in my life were higher than anything I had ever experienced before. I was exhausted beyond all comprehension and was very close to breaking point...

I lacked energy and motivation in contacting friends and family

Learning from Seattle

One of my favourite films is *Sleepless in Seattle* with Tom Hanks and Meg Ryan. A real weepy, it is the story of a young widower called Sam who finds love again with a stranger through a series of occurrences strategically masterminded and arranged by his young son, Jonah. Initially, Jonah secretly telephones a radio chat show and asks the guest doctor to help find a new partner for his father. Eventually, Sam is encouraged to speak on the live phone-in show about the impact of grief and bereavement. Asked how he will cope, he says, 'I'm going to get out of bed every morning, breathe in and out all day long, and then after a while I won't have to remind myself to get out of bed

in the morning and breathe in and out.'

Perhaps the greatest surprise for me in the aftermath of losing Clare was just how exhausting grief can be. I was completely unprepared for the impact of the overwhelming tiredness I felt... This exhaustion had four primary ramifications for my day-to-day activities.

First, my sleep patterns became erratic in the extreme. I simply could not face going to bed alone so I would either lie there listening to the radio all night or else sleep on the sofa downstairs... I would watch TV into the small hours and would be doing the housework or some academic research as the sun rose.

Second, the exhaustion of grief resulted in a lack of energy for even the most basic tasks. Work-related activities that would previously have taken an hour of my time now filled an entire day. My levels of concentration became so low that I would be able to spend only five or ten minutes at a particular assignment before wandering off to make yet another cup of coffee or switching on daytime TV. My short-term memory became seriously deficient and so I was constantly having to recover the details of schedules and work responsibilities or else apologize profusely to those who had been let down by my failure to remember appointments and arrangements.

Third, I lacked energy and

motivation in contacting friends and family. Even the shortest of conversations left me exhausted and depressed... I was tired of having to tell people over and over again in a single day how I was getting on... Eventually, it became easier just to say, 'I'm fine, thanks', even though I was aware that this response led others to believe I was in some sort of denial.

Fourth, I found myself becoming extremely discerning about how to spend what little time and energy reserves I had within me. Never one for making much small talk with strangers, I now found myself not bothering to interact on a superficial level at all, and, uncharacteristically, not even caring if others thought of me as rude. I reasoned that I had little enough energy to survive the day and was not prepared to expend any on shallow personal interaction... I had become acutely aware that there is no time to waste in life. Every moment of my existence had to be lived to its full potential, and I was not about to allow anybody to rob me of whatever living I had left to do.

Most frightening of all was the stark realization that I was constantly on the edge of doing something very stupid. I do not mean suicide: the thought has never crossed my mind. For a long time after losing Clare, however, the anguish of grief bred a subconscious desire in me to 'self-destruct'. I was aware that just one little push would send me over the precipice. Sometimes I even wanted to be pushed. There were days when I would deliberately become antagonistic so that I could force an argument. Then, when I was alone that evening, I would have an excuse to feel sorry for myself and could seek comfort in a few glasses too many of Jack Daniels... Like Sam in *Sleepless in Seattle*, I could not see beyond getting out of bed in the morning and reminding myself to take the next breath.

The first step towards receiving healing in grief was an intensely

I was exhausted beyond all comprehension and was very close to breaking point

pragmatic one. I had to learn to look after Number One on a physical and emotional level before I could allow God to tend my spiritual wounds. This is not as selfish or 'unspiritual' as it may sound. Indeed, this pragmatic approach is an entirely biblical one, as the story of Elijah shows.

The experience of grief is often akin to that of wind, earthquake and fire in the soul

Look after Number One

1 Kings 19 is a well-known part of scripture, primarily for the description of the manifestation of God in 'the soft whisper of a voice' (v. 12). Important though this description of the activity of God is, the central theme of the chapter is not so much the theophany as Elijah's call to ministry. In terms reminiscent of so many Old Testament encounters between a prophet and God, Elijah is brought from self-doubt to a place of recommissioning in ministry...

Elijah had been on Mount Carmel, engaged in a colossal confrontation with the prophets of Baal. The reputation of the Lord God was at stake in this conflict. In the presence of hundreds of Israelites, 450 prophets of

Baal and 400 prophets of the goddess Asherah, Elijah had performed a miracle that vindicated the existence and power of his God...

In that one triumphant moment, Elijah had discredited the powers of darkness, challenged the political and spiritual leaders of the nation and vindicated the power and authenticity of his own prophetic ministry. Queen Jezebel, the wife of the reigning King Ahab, was so infuriated and embarrassed by this incident that she sent a threatening message to Elijah... This threat from the queen was the incident that triggered Elijah's subsequent collapse.

In truth, Elijah was absolutely exhausted following his exertions on Mount Carmel. In that power encounter, he had given everything he possibly could. He was physically, emotionally and spiritually drained and, as a result, was unable to retain any perspective on the unfolding events. The threat that Jezebel had made threw Elijah into a state of overwhelming anxiety. We read in verse 3 that 'Elijah was afraid' and that his only thought was to escape by running away. Interestingly, it was not the reality of his present situation that caused Elijah to fall victim to fear and depression. Rather, it was fear of the future; fear of what torment might befall him at the hands of the queen. For a moment in time, Elijah ceased contemplation of the awesome, miraculous power of the God whom he served and became preoccupied instead with possible futures. The

Hebrew in verse 3 that is translated 'Elijah was afraid' actually reads, 'Elijah sees how things are'. But the truth is that Elijah did not see how things were at all! Instead, he feared how things might turn out to be. As a result of stress and fear, Elijah had stopped discerning 'spiritually' and had begun merely reacting to the circumstances of life. Elijah was motivated to flee for his life because of his own assessment of the situation. He was not following a word from the Lord. Indeed, the path he followed stood in absolute contradiction to the will of God. Elijah fled to the furthest point south—Beersheba in Judah—but later, in verse 15, God would instruct him to go north again!

Verses 3 and 4 are deeply insightful, with so much information about the psychology of Elijah being revealed in the detail of the story. First, we are told, 'Leaving the servant there, Elijah walked a whole day into the wilderness.' There are two things to note here. In leaving his servant behind, Elijah was symbolically renouncing his prophetic ministry. His servant would have been his helper, freeing Elijah from domestic considerations to devote himself to his divine calling. By ridding himself of that helpmate, Elijah was acknowledging his belief that he no longer had a part to play in the purposes of God. Also, by leaving Beersheba and going into the wilderness, Elijah was effectively divorcing himself from the covenant people of God. His depression was such that he could not countenance living out an existence within the context of faith-relationships. There was no one to help him. There was no one who could possibly understand how he felt...

There is something intensely poignant about the description of this lonely, tortured soul detailed in verse 4. The tree under which he sat was a 'broom-brush'... a tree growing to a height of over three metres. We can picture him sitting under this single

Elijah was symbolically renouncing his prophetic ministry

Elijah is brought from self-doubt to a place of recommissioning **in ministry**

tree in the wilderness seeking shade from the intense heat of the sun, utterly alone, contemplating death. There was nothing logical about his state of depression. After all, he had just experienced remarkable success on Mount Carmel and had witnessed the awesome power of his God. But the truth is that there is no logic in

I had become acutely aware that there is no time to waste in life

depression. Elijah was clearly disorientated and confused. In verse 3, we read that 'Elijah was afraid, and fled for his life.' In verse 4, he prays the exact opposite desire to God: 'Take away my life; I might as well be dead!' That oscillation between the innate desire to survive and the inclination to give up and die is not unusual for those suffering depression. For those afflicted by grief, this alternation between the determination to endure and the tendency to quit may happen not only on a day-by-day basis but even hourly.

Elijah was burnt out. Verse 5 starkly states, 'He lay down under the tree and fell asleep', but in that most natural response to fatigue began the process of his holistic restoration. God allowed

him to slumber for a while before taking the initiative in sending an angel. It is interesting to note that, at this stage, the angel did not bring any spiritually profound message from the Lord. Rather, there was a gracious gentleness in his instruction: 'Wake up and eat' (v. 5). Elijah partook of the water and bread. Thereafter, the process of physical healing was allowed to continue as he went back to sleep.

Some time later, the angel of the Lord visited Elijah for a second time. There was a subtle difference to this visit, even though it was still manifestly compassionate. On this occasion, the angel woke Elijah and said, 'Get up and eat, or the journey will be too much for you' (v. 7). Here, there is a twofold emphasis on the beginning of a recommissioning to ministry. First, Elijah was encouraged to 'get up', rather than just 'wake up'. There was something more proactive required of him at this point. Second, there was mention of a journey upon which Elijah would soon be asked to embark. The emphasis was still on physical recuperation but there was the promise of a journey. Elijah had thought that his journey was finished in the wilderness but God had other ideas. The angel did not give any detail about where the journey would lead. He just gave hope that Elijah's present situation was not the end... God was gently restoring Elijah, physically and emotionally—in that order—before engaging him spiritually in active ministry once more.

In verse 8, we read of his response: 'Elijah got up, ate and drank, and the food gave him enough strength to walk forty days to Sinai, the holy mountain.' ... Upon arriving at Sinai, he went into a cave and spent the night there (v. 9). This period of rest marked the completion of this phase of Elijah's restoration. God had physically restored him through sleep, food and drink. God had emotionally restored him through the promise of a journey to a destination of the Lord's choosing. Having arrived at that destination, Elijah now became spiritually restored as he spent the night meditating and praying in a cave. Having been restored physically, emotionally and spiritually, Elijah was now ready to be met by God in a profoundly personal manner.

The detail of that meeting with God is not our primary concern here. Suffice it to note only that God was not to be found in the furious wind or the earthquake or the fire. Instead, God was to be found in 'the soft whisper of a voice' (v. 12). There are two things to note here. First, the experience of grief is often akin to that of wind, earthquake and fire in the soul. We feel tossed and blown around, victim to the elements. We feel torn asunder, with the very heart of our being ripped out from within us. We feel burnt by the flames that lick the depths of our being. But the promise of God is that the force of these uncontrollable circumstances will be replaced by a gentle encounter with the living, gracious, compassionate God. The nature of that encounter is not an impersonal one. We are encountered by a voice—the voice of our Father whose care and concern is for our whole being, mind, body and spirit. As with Elijah, he promises to restore us to wholeness.

The exhaustion and depression that grief causes is by no means the end of our usefulness in the ministry and service of our God. The all-consuming weariness that so often accompanies bereavement is not the end of the journey. Rather, God would have us

Many of us will experience involuntary times of confinement

respond pragmatically. Sleep; eat; drink. Only then will we be in a position to hear the gracious calling of God on our lives. Only then will we be strong enough to work with God in the restoring of our spirituality. There is nothing selfish in pragmatic spirituality. The message of this story about Elijah, in the context of moving through the experience of grief is disarmingly simple: look after Number One. ■

Bible quotations are from the GNB.

An adventure is only an inconvenience rightly considered.
An inconvenience is only an adventure wrongly considered.
G.K. CHESTERTON (1874–1936), 'ALL THINGS CONSIDERED'

I went to the woods because I wished to live deliberately,
to front only the essential facts of life, and see if I could not learn
what it had to teach, and not, when I came to die,
discover that I had not lived.
HENRY DAVID THOREAU (1817-62), 'WALDEN'

It is such a secret place, the land of tears.
ANTOINE DE SAINT-EXUPÉRY (1900-44), 'THE LITTLE PRINCE'

Man cannot discover new oceans
unless he has the courage
to lose sight of the shore.
ANDRÉ GIDE, 1869-1951

What would the world be, once bereft of wet and wildness?
GERARD MANLEY HOPKINS (1844–89)

And now in age I bud again,
After so many deaths I live and write;
I once more smell the dew and rain,
And relish versing: O my only Light,
It cannot be
That I am he
On whom Thy tempests fell all night.
GEORGE HERBERT (1593–1633), 'THE FLOWER'

Retreats
in the desert

The Revd Dr Emma Loveridge is founder and director of Wind, Sand & Stars Ltd, which takes people on guided journeys to the Sinai. The company also works with the local nomadic Bedu tribes, providing direct trade in keeping with their cultural lifestyle to alleviate poverty, as well as running developmental projects.

It is hard to imagine that anyone has been this way before as you lie in your sleeping bag, looking up at the clear, starlit night sky after a day ambling gently on camelback through the valleys that wend their way between the golden sandstone hills. Yet it is part of an ancient Christian pilgrim route following the famous stories of Moses. Others, less well-known, have also walked here in the last 2000 years to the site where Mount Sinai is now located, as well as to the still-active sixth-century walled monastery of St Catherine with its unique art treasures and manuscript library in the shadow of the great red granite mountain.

Many people ask, 'Is it really Mount Sinai?' Mount Sinai is named in the book of Exodus, where the story of the Ten Commandments is told, and centuries later it is also the place where Elijah hid in a cave after fleeing from wicked Queen Jezebel. The prophet sought God in the earthquake, wind and fire and finally found him in the 'still small voice of calm'.

Space for silence and freedom to think

45

The journey and the mountain are a symbol of our journey through life

This well-known phrase, however, translates better from the original verse in the book of 1 Kings as the 'crushing silence'. Such a translation also typifies the depth of silence found only in the very heart of a desert.

I wholeheartedly believe that the answer to 'Is it the real Mount Sinai?' is both 'yes' and 'no'—a working paradox, if you like. If you want the scholarly answer, then it is almost certainly 'no'. The mountain is impossible to locate from the biblical texts,

and if you could find it, it would almost certainly lie in the barren north of the Sinai peninsula, not in this beautiful, oasis-filled mountain range in the south. However, I believe the answer is also 'yes' if you are a Christian pilgrim, because the outer journey reflects the inner journey of a pilgrim seeking the presence of God. The journey and the mountain are a symbol of our journey through life, where we seek to know and understand ourselves better in a relationship with God. The mountain, which Christians have named as Mount Sinai, has become a symbol of the presence of God amid the wider journey of life—a place where ancient stories are reinterpreted for our own lives; a place to meet God. In this sense, the answer is 'yes': for us, as pilgrims, it is indeed Mount Sinai.

So we move from pilgrimage to retreat. As well as offering ancient temples on hilltops and monasteries tucked away in secret valleys, the desert and mountains of Sinai are also the home of the honourable and hospitable Bedouin tribes. Their longstanding relationship with Wind, Sand & Stars gives us the opportunity to spend time in one place in the desert, with Bedu families as our hosts, offering space for silence and freedom to think, unfettered by city life. The wind-eroded latticework in the sandstone hillsides gives the setting a unique beauty, and the desert silence cannot be explained to those who have not experienced it. The mixture of talks and companionship with space for silence and solitude has been appreciated hugely by many who desire company in their Christian journey, yet are crying out for time to be free to wait on God.

There is something about companionship, tribal wisdom and the rhythm of life set by the rising and dying of the sun that creates a space for regeneration. Such regeneration can be desperately lacking in our urban-based societies, which

The rhythm of life set by the rising and dying of the sun

whittle away the corners where human nature finds its vitally needed recovery from the day, and the moments where relationships are forged and God enters into the fray with our knowledge, perhaps even our permission.

I was once privileged to translate a conversation between a young pilgrim and a local desert holy man. I tell the story of that conversation here through the eyes of the holy man, as it seems to me that it celebrates in many ways the compassionate ambiguity that I believe to be at the heart of desert retreats. In the desert silence, the challenge of grappling with self-conflict and, at the same time, the restorative process invariably walk side by side.

It was some years ago when a boy sat by my side one evening in the early summer. He didn't come from here; he came from far away, from a green land. Suddenly he spoke to me. He wanted to know

The depth of silence found only in the very **heart of a desert**

When times were hard I could speak of God and return him to the hearts of the tribe

why the others called me the 'holy man'—what had made me the holy man among my cousins here. I was silent as I fed the fire. Why was I the holy man? I was silent and rinsed the glasses for tea. What made me different from the others in my family? I was silent still. I opened my pouch for the sugar and took a long time to untie the string.

He asked again. 'Did you go away to learn to be a holy man?' I felt I should answer something. His eyes were steady, honest, and the

blueness, which I was so unused to, held me. Did he not know that in this life what you have and who you are comes from God? But I saw no jest in the unfamiliarity of his features. So I told him. 'It came from God.' We were silent again and the strong desert wind made us draw up nearer the fire.

As the wind drove the chill of the desert night through our clothes, the boy suddenly cursed the wind. The sand, he said, was stinging his eyes. I felt it too, but I knew that as the sun rose tomorrow the wind would be God's gift to us. I told the boy gently. 'Don't think of the wind in this way, for tomorrow, if it stays with us through the heat, it will be God's blessing upon us.'

We all knew the wind came from God, the bitter chill that sent the old to him and the summer north breeze in which the children grew tall. My grandfather had known these things, my mother also, and now my children learned them, so why was I the holy man among my people? Perhaps because I could speak of the things from God. Like now, I was the only one to tell the boy, the only one to see he didn't know these things. Perhaps my people thought I had the gift of God in my heart and on my lips. When times were hard I could speak of God and return him to the hearts of the tribe. Perhaps that was why I was the holy man.

I told him of my birth. I was the fourth child to be born in my family, the second son. I was small and weak, with ankles like matches, and marked by death. The weakness grew worse and my mother tells me I should not have lived. But by the grace of God I did. It was from this day I was called holy. It was a very part of my nature. God had given me the gift of life, and I had grown and brought God into the lives of others by my presence.

The boy looked at me closely; he wanted to know more. He asked carefully. Had I become a wise and holy man because my family had called me so, or would God have called me to be a holy man anyway, and would I have responded?

I understood his question but I had no answer. So I told him the truth: I do not know the answer. He asked me who had called me to show the presence of God—my people, myself or God. So I gave him another answer. My people and I have always known I was called to be close to God. It is a gift.

I handed him a cigarette and we smoked, hunched over against the chill. His blue eyes were lost in the darkness, his body cramped by the wind so foreign to him, and his mind bewildered by a story without an end or a beginning.

I knew that as the sun rose tomorrow the wind would be God's gift to us

Why do they call me a holy man? Who called me?

In the morning the boy would stand tall again because of the wind. As it cooled him from the burning sun and swept the flies away from his skin, he would know that on this night he had been blessed by God. I wondered if he would ask where the gift of the wind came from and why it came to him. I thought it unlikely. I would probably never see this boy again as he left my land, but I asked God to bring him blessings every year. ■

For more information about the retreats and pilgrimages run by Wind Sand & Stars, visit www.windsandstars.co.uk, email office@windsandstars.co.uk or phone 020 7359 7551.

A beachcomber

We are like misshapen pieces of wood:
a stealthy configuration
floating under a limitless moon,
or ambushed by a tide that washes
against the edge of the noon.

We spend ourselves in fruitless labour
which our own hearts oppose.
There is neither profit nor pleasure,
neither relish nor leisure,
amongst the detritus of the shallows.
Whilst our lives form and re-form
our cry is: 'Useless! Useless!'
Like the seagull's lament,
it competes for a hearing
with the waves, the veering
west wind and the storm.

But Jesus is a beachcomber.
He walks where sand and water mingle,
retrieving flotsam from the eddying foam.
He bends down low to take
jetsam from the shingle,
knowing what it will signify,
looking at it with an artist's eye,
holding it in his hands and taking it home.

Whatever he saves from the ravage
of the pitiless ebb and flow
and the savage assault of the sea
he transforms into something carefree.

JUDITH PINHEY, FROM 'THE SONG OF HOPE' (BRF, 2002)

St Brendan
the Navigator

Emma Garrow is a freelance writer and a longstanding contributor to 'The Church of England Newspaper'.

St Brendan is reputed by legend to be the first person to have discovered America. Icons of this sixth-century Irish saint, known as 'Brendan the Navigator', feature him with the curragh or boat in which he is said to have sailed across the Atlantic. He is also depicted with a monastic building, a reference to his life's work as the founder of monastic communities in western Ireland and the west of Scotland.

The legend of Brendan's most dramatic journey suggests that he was already in his 70s when he set sail to find 'Paradise'—a journey that, according to the earliest record of the legend, the tenth-century *Navigatio Sancti Brendani*, lasted seven years.

The inspiration for Brendan's journey was twofold. Looking out across the waters of the Atlantic one day, he saw a vision of the 'Land of Promises'. Shortly after this, he received a visitor, who staggered in, claiming to have just that minute returned from a voyage to that very land. Brendan sensed a calling. He got together a group of 16 monks and set about building a curragh that would take them to this wonderful destination.

> The medieval hearers of the tale believed in the existence of 'St Brendan's Isle'

The journey was fraught with many dangers. The travellers landed on an island that turned out to be a whale, which nearly drowned them when they built a cooking-fire upon its back. They passed an island of crystal pillars from which lumps of fiery rock descended

Celtic Christians sought the 'desert in the ocean'

Severin's journey makes Brendan's legend seem less outlandish

on to their little boat. They went round in circles several times before they finally reached their destination, and all this on initial provisions for only 40 days, in a vessel directed by the wind alone.

Yet sustenance was provided amid the hardship and danger. The whale turned friendly, permitting the monks to celebrate the Easter Eucharist on its back once a year. An island of birds provided food, rest and water, sending the pilgrims off at Pentecost with replenished supplies and a prophecy: God would continue to provide for them at key points in the church calendar until 'the seven years of your pilgrimage will be ended'.

Everything transpired accordingly. Brendan and his companions reached the 'Land of Promises', wandering its reaches until they came to a great river that they could not cross, keeping them 'ignorant of the size of this country'. Upon leaving, they were granted to take fruits as nourishment and precious stones as evidence of their success.

Brendan's story may sound far-fetched with its talking birds and obliging whales, but, put in context, it has a ring of truth. Celtic monks such as Brendan were spiritual descendants of the Desert Fathers, who sought the wilderness as a place to seek God free from the distractions of the world. Lacking a desert land, Celtic Christians sought the 'desert in the ocean', which they accessed in curraghs, vulnerable wicker shells covered in hide and tar and navigated by means of a sail alone.

We know that Brendan employed curraghs throughout his life and ministry because he founded monasteries across the western shores of the British Isles. Brendan was part of the tradition of those great Celtic saints who loved to journey for God, allowing their physical travels to bear witness to the inner life of the soul. These pilgrimages were embarked upon with a clear destination in mind. Brendan began his legendary voyage as a result of a vision of paradise and the testimony of a fellow traveller. His inspiration for braving the terrors of the unknown was a deep faith and a love for God, which enabled him to hear God's call to him across the wilderness.

Throughout their journey, as the *Navigatio Sancti Brendani* makes clear, Brendan and his monks continued to observe monastic practice, celebrating the rites and festivals of the liturgical year. In this way, Brendan kept the focus of his pilgrimage always on God, gaining courage from the act of worship. Brendan and his companions had voluntarily embarked upon a pilgrimage to the kind of wilderness described in Psalm 107, where they saw for themselves 'the works of the Lord, his wonderful deeds in the deep' (v. 24).

Sustenance
was provided amid the hardship and danger

Modern fascination with the story of St Brendan has focused on whether or not he really was the first to reach America. Certainly the medieval hearers of the tale believed in the existence of 'St Brendan's Isle', as maps of that period reveal. In 1976, a British navigation scholar, Tim Severin, undertook a study to ascertain the likelihood of the story. He built a curragh and set sail with the wind as his guide. His experiences suggest that the details in the *Navigatio Sancti Brendani* are drawn from possible realities. Severin passed islands where Irish monks had certainly founded monasteries. He encountered friendly whales, swimming around his boat as if it were a companion on their own travels.

Following the wind, Severin sailed past the island of Mykines, home to thousands of sea birds. He wintered in Iceland, where he realized that both the volcanic activity and the icebergs there would have been outrageous novelties to a band of sixth-century Irish pilgrims far from home.

Several months after setting sail, Severin reached Newfoundland, Canada. Could this have been Brendan's 'Land of Promise'? No one can know for sure, but Severin's journey makes Brendan's legend seem less outlandish. If true, it means that Brendan and his companions crossed hitherto unknown boundaries in their search for God. Their passion for knowing the divine inspired them to choose the wilderness in response to the call of God to live in him. ∎

Survival Kit

Naomi Starkey is the editor of 'Quiet Spaces'. She also edits 'New Daylight' Bible reading notes, as well as commissioning BRF's range of books for adults.

My dad loved the idea of wild places. On family holidays we never stayed on campsites but parked our VW van wherever there was a convenient and more-or-less level piece of ground (lacking—shall we say—washroom facilities), usually in a remote part of the Scottish Highlands. While I heard rumours that other families spent time relaxing on beaches, we paddled across sea lochs (breaking the ice first in winter time), climbed large

mountains, and from time to time got told to move on by irate landowners.

As a way of developing this general frontier mentality in us, my brother and I were given a special present one day: a book for Young People about how to survive in all kinds of hostile situations. We spent many entertaining hours learning how to break the grip of an assailant, how to cross flooded terrain on a bicycle, how to produce water out of thin air with an assortment of mirrors and plastic bags.

Best of all were the instructions for building a survival kit. Believe it or not, it is possible to fit the essentials for providing light, shelter, nourishment and way-finding all in a container the size of a fountain pen. Thus equipped, the Young Person would never be at a loss even when dropped into the most arduous of wilderness situations.

I can't say we ever persevered with the survival kit, although we had fun magnetizing needles, coiling fuse wire round birthday cake candles (to make them burn more slowly) and trying to devise a rainproof shelter with a handful of leafy branches and string. And despite the holidays spent camping rough, we never did get to the point of having to 'survive'. At the end of it all, our parents were always there to drive us home.

As I grew older, however, I realized two things. One was that there were many young people who, in different countries and at different times, really did (and still do) have to survive completely on their own. For them, survival was no game but a deadly serious way of life, on city streets, in war zones, in drought-stricken and disease-ravaged countryside. This realization put into perspective my gripes about a lack of hot showers and having to eat breakfast cereal with lukewarm long-life milk.

What I also realized was that there are many kinds of wilderness. Some of these 'places' may be materially comfortable and familiar but emotionally and spiritually desolate. Rather than a fortnight spent walking in a scenically splendid part of Britain, 'living outside the comfort zone' could mean having to move house, a change of career path that involves loss in status and money, enduring a crushingly difficult work or home situation, bereavement, ill health, profound disappointment...

Entering the adult world meant recognizing that some people have to endure some kinds of wildernesses for months, if not years. And these wildernesses may offer little by way of relief for those who have to sojourn

Even the smallest of flames has the potential to kindle a great fire

there. There is no mountain-top view to reward the one who toils painfully up a never-ending slope, no glacier-fed stream to refresh the tired trekker.

Of course, some of these wilderness situations may be entered voluntarily, responding to a call from God—a clear sense that there is really only one choice to be made, and that is the hard one. People may set out into a personal wilderness with a clear sense of the rightness of what they are about to undergo—but the experience can still frequently be exhausting and dispiriting.

We need to learn how to protect ourselves prayerfully

Somebody may know that they are called to a particular job or undertaking, and they may maintain a deep sense of security that they are living in obedience to God, but even so there will be times when they want to give up and 'go home', retreat to the comfort zone where all the rest lead peaceful and contented lives.

So how can we cope? How do we maintain the mental and emotional energy to continue along our path, whether we are travelling there willingly or unwillingly, whether it consists of a demanding relationship, a painful physical condition or living in a difficult neighbourhood? Is there a spiritual survival kit that can provide the essentials of shelter, warmth and nourishment to keep us going in our wilderness time?

Remembering my attempts to be a surviving Young Person, with vital bits of equipment crammed into the pen-sized container, here are some suggestions for the spiritual survival kit.

The shelter/God's comforting presence

Whether it is a hi-tech mountain tent or an emergency plastic sheet, we need to have shelter when we are out in the wild places. Psalm 121 paints a vivid picture of God's comforting presence, shading us from the heat of the day and guarding us against night-time dangers.

The magnetized needle/God's guidance

The magnetized needle, hanging on a thread, spins round to point north, indicating the way to go. Exodus 40:36–38 tells how God led the people of Israel through the desert as a pillar of cloud and of fire. If we try to travel without God's guidance, we can all too easily end up lost, wandering in circles and fearing that there is no escape. If we are willing to follow him, God will show us the path to take.

Glucose tablets/energy for the task

The act of surviving can use up a great deal of energy, because tasks that normally require little or no thought—getting a drink of water, for example—can take on huge significance and require vast effort in the wilderness context. As glucose tablets provide instant energy, so we need to know what brings us an instant refuel of emotional energy—a phone call to a friend, a walk in the park, an 'arrow prayer', something simple that 'restores our soul' (Psalm 23:3).

Knife blade/protection

A sharp knife, even a very small blade, can be a useful survival tool and, if necessary, a defensive weapon. When we are in our personal wilderness, we need to learn how to protect ourselves prayerfully. We may need to learn the defensive art of saying 'no' to others' requests, of not taking on more than we can handle. And we may need to resist the voice of the accuser, 'the devil... like a roaring lion, looking for someone to devour' (1 Peter 5:8–9), tempting us to give in to despair and abandon the struggle to keep going.

String/the bonds of love

As string literally holds all manner of things in place, making useful what may otherwise be useless, so love 'binds... all together in perfect unity' (Colossians 3:14). Just as some kind of string is an essential item in the survival kit, so we need love to hold ourselves together in our own survival situation. We need to nurture our love for God, for whoever else is in the situation with us, and for ourselves.

Candle/the power of the Holy Spirit

I described how, in the original plan for a survival kit, the light source was a birthday cake candle bound with fuse wire to make it burn more slowly (plus a few waterproof matches). Even if it is tiny, a light can bring warmth, hope and clarity of vision, and even the smallest of flames has the potential to kindle a great fire. As Christians, we are promised the help of God's Holy Spirit, who came to the disciples at Pentecost like tongues of fire (Acts 2:3), bringing a previously unimaginable strength to help them through the challenges that lay ahead, challenges that included the most arduous of wilderness times.

Of course there is always more that can be usefully added—both to the survival kit for the real-life wilderness trail and to the 'survival kit' for whatever spiritual desert we may be

> **Some people have to endure some kinds of wildernesses for months, if not years**

enduring, but sometimes it is helpful to think about what might constitute the essentials. With the essentials in place, we can at least keep going, one foot in front of the other, trusting that we are travelling in the right direction. We can endure the wilderness storms because we have shelter and protection. And we can continue in hope, knowing that we have enough to sustain us until rescue comes—or we find the way through to whatever lies beyond. ∎

The wilderness

These prayers are written by speaker and author Celia Bowring. Celia writes for 'Day by Day with God' Bible reading notes and compiles the CARE Prayer Guide. Her recent book, 'We're In This Together' (Authentic, 2006) is about and for women married to Christian leaders. She is married to Lyndon and they have two sons and a daughter.

Immediately after being baptized by John and commissioned by the Father to begin his ministry, Jesus withdrew into the desert for 40 days and nights. Our prayers through the week reflect on this experience.

Sunday

Jesus… returned from the Jordan and was led by the Spirit in the wilderness (Luke 4:1).

Loving Lord, help us to recognize those times when you are calling us aside, to be quiet, away from the hurly-burly of activity and the people who normally surround us—whether by our own choice or through separation, suffering or sickness. Holy Spirit, please speak to us in our desert places and shape us more into the likeness of Jesus.

Here I am, Father. Sometimes I feel vulnerable and uncertain of the way ahead, but in faith I look to you for all I need, for as long as it takes, to journey through this wilderness where you lead me. Amen.

Monday

He ate nothing during those days, and at the end of them he was hungry (Luke 4:2, NIV).

Heavenly Father, millions of people today will wake up starving and lie down again tonight still with nothing to eat. With all our hearts we pray that nourishing food and clean water will be provided for them. We are so grateful for all that we have and we want to share with others, however we can.

O Lord, sometimes I feel so hungry. In the wilderness you sent down manna and made water gush from the rock to satisfy those who depended on you. Help me to look to you for my needs, not to look elsewhere for help— especially in the hard times. Amen.

Tuesday

'People do not live on bread alone, but on every word that comes from the mouth of God' (Matthew 4:4, NIV).

O God, thank you for the pure truth and life-giving power of your word— more precious than gold and sweeter than honey. Our world desperately needs to acknowledge your sovereignty. We pray for many more people to come humbly before you and receive the gift of salvation through Jesus Christ our Lord.

Holy Spirit, please speak into my life through the Bible today. May its words be alive and active, sharper than a double-edged sword to penetrate the deepest thoughts and attitudes of my mind and heart. Show me what is right, and inspire and comfort me, especially in the wilderness times. Amen.

Wednesday

The tempter came to him and said… (Matthew 4:3, NIV).

We praise you, Jesus, for rescuing us from the power of sin, death and the devil. You fight for us against our evil adversary who desires our downfall, exploiting us in the desert places of our lives.

Father, please forgive me and help me when I fail. Lift up my head to see your love and grace at work in me in every situation. Teach me to put on the full spiritual armour that your Spirit provides, to stand my ground with courage and strength when trials come. Thank you for the promise that you will provide a way of escape and I will not be tested beyond what I can bear. Amen.

Thursday

'Worship the Lord your God, and serve him only' (Luke 4:10, NIV).

Good Shepherd, we are sorry for the times when we do not follow you, when we get a bit lost and confused by other voices, and take the wrong direction. Please guide us through the narrow gateway that leads to heaven, and strengthen our hearts to seek your kingdom and righteousness first.

Dear Lord Jesus, some days in the wilderness I lose sight of the truth that you alone are the way, and do not worship and serve you as you deserve. Pour out your grace upon me and soften my heart. Please illuminate the path ahead and grant me the incomparable peace and joy that comes from knowing you. Amen.

Friday

'He will command his angels concerning you, and they will lift you up in their hands'... Jesus answered him, '... Do not put the Lord your God to the test' (Matthew 4:6–7, NIV).

Thank you, Lord Jesus, for your sacrificial love. Even when the devil tempted you to distrust your Father's provision, challenge his plan and doubt

his protection, you stayed faithful all the way to the cross. Please draw close to anyone today who is in a wilderness of uncertainty, and send your angels to encourage them.

Father, I trust that all things will work together for my good. Allow whatever is necessary to accomplish your will in my life and please help me to walk close beside you through it all. Amen.

Saturday

Jesus returned to Galilee in the power of the Spirit, and news about him spread through the whole countryside (Luke 4:14, NIV).

Almighty God, thank you for those wilderness experiences that make us strong. We praise you for everyone serving you, all those who trust in you, reflect your glory and bring honour to your name. Let them be increasingly fruitful in everything they do for you.

Jesus, please deepen my love and knowledge of you day by day. May I always bless your name—both in good times and desert places. Send me out in the power of the Holy Spirit to serve you with all I am and in all I do. Amen.

Musings of a middle-aged mystic

Veronica Zundel is a journalist, author and contributor to BRF's 'New Daylight' Bible reading notes. She lives in north London.

Have you heard of Achsah? She was one of the obscure biblical women I highlighted in a recent seminar at the Greenbelt festival (see Joshua 15). The daughter of Caleb, she was promised by her father in marriage to whoever conquered the town of Kiriath-sepher. As it happened, Othniel, Caleb's nephew, took the town; so Achsah was married to her cousin. Her own views are not recorded.

Now here's the bit that interests me. Apparently, Caleb had given the young couple a wedding present of some land. Unfortunately, it was in the Negev—which, as you probably know, is a desert. So Achsah began to nag her husband to ask her father for a field. He must have replied, 'Go and ask him yourself', for the next we hear, she is getting off her donkey and saying to Caleb, 'Since you have given me land in the desert, give me also springs of water.' And her fond father gives her two springs. This shows that she had thought it over, and realized that a constant source of irrigation would be more use than a mere field.

There are lessons that we can only learn in the wilderness

> **Life is so powerful that it doesn't need much water to get it springing up again**

I haven't been to the Negev myself, but I have been on the road from Jerusalem to Jericho, and to the Dead Sea, so I have some idea what a Middle Eastern desert looks like. It was a stroke of genius on Jesus' part to set the story of the good heretic (as I call it) on the Jericho road. Those barren yellow hills are a fine hide-out for muggers.

Is the desert, or wilderness, merely the place of loneliness, danger and fear? Is it the land where nothing lives? When we are 'in the wilderness' spiritually, is that just a break in our growth?

Many years ago, I read the book *Poustinia* by Catherine de Hueck Doherty. *Poustinia* is Russian for 'wilderness', and the book told of the Orthodox tradition of deliberately seeking out a 'desert place' in which to draw closer to God.

I was attracted to this idea, but didn't know how to take it further. Then one day on *Songs of Praise*, I heard an interviewee talk about going to a 'poustinia hut' at The Grail retreat centre in north London. I promptly looked up The Grail, and became, for a while, a regular visitor to their simple but comfortable huts for a night or two. To be honest, these 'lodges' are set in a garden, not a desert, but they fulfil the 'desert' requirement in the sense that they are quiet, solitary, and offer undisturbed time in silence and meditation.

Those huts, and other places of quiet retreat, became for me a lifeline in my over-busy city life. I can't quantify it, but I believe that spiritual growth took place there for me. Maybe you've had one of those little cactus-like plants called bromeliads, or 'air plants', set in a scallop shell or a little bottle, which were fashionable about 20 years ago. They don't need earth or water, just an occasional spray of moisture. They live on what's in the air. Literal deserts are actually full of hidden life (and not just muggers). Perhaps the same is true for our own spiritual deserts: perhaps there are lessons that we can only learn in the wilderness, growth that can only happen there.

Achsah's demand to her father became a key verse for me in my single years, which often felt like a desert. I asked God for 'springs of water', and I believe God gave them. Life is so powerful that it doesn't need much water to get it springing up again; even between city paving stones, grass can grow. ■

We want to hear from you...

Thank you to all our readers who have contacted us over the past months. It has been so encouraging to hear your thoughts about *Quiet Spaces* and to see the fruits of your creativity. If you have access to the Internet, do please visit the *Quiet Spaces* website: www.quietspaces.org.uk.

In the next issue, we consider 'The City'. The Bible starts in a garden, but ends in a heavenly city, where all nations walk by the light of God's glory. We will celebrate the human creativity and diversity that 'city' signifies, and reflect on some of the challenges of city living.

Contact us at:

Quiet Spaces,
BRF, First Floor,
Elsfield Hall,
15–17 Elsfield Way,
Oxford OX2 8FG

enquiries@brf.org.uk

QUIET SPACES SUBSCRIPTIONS

Quiet Spaces is published three times a year, in March, July and November. To take out a subscription, please complete this form, indicating the month in which you would like your subscription to begin.

☐ I would like to give a gift subscription (please complete both name and address sections below)

☐ I would like to take out a subscription myself (complete name and address details only once)

This completed coupon should be sent with appropriate payment to BRF. Alternatively, please write to us quoting your name, address, the subscription you would like for either yourself or a friend (with their name and address), the start date and credit card number, expiry date and signature if paying by credit card.

Gift subscription name _____

Gift subscription address _____

_____

_____ Postcode _____

Please send beginning with the next November / March / July issue: *(delete as applicable)*

(please tick box)	UK	SURFACE	AIR MAIL
Quiet Spaces	☐ £16.95	☐ £18.45	☐ £20.85

Please complete the payment details below and send your coupon, with appropriate payment to: BRF, First Floor, Elsfield Hall, 15–17 Elsfield Way, Oxford OX2 8FG.

Name _____

Address _____

_____

Postcode _____ Telephone Number _____

Email _____

☐ Please do not email me any information about BRF publications

Method of payment: ☐ Cheque ☐ Mastercard ☐ Visa ☐ Postal Order ☐ Switch

Card no. ☐☐☐☐ ☐☐☐☐ ☐☐☐☐ ☐☐☐☐ ☐☐☐☐

Expires ☐☐ ☐☐ Issue no. of Switch card ☐☐☐

Signature _____ Date ____/____/____

All orders must be accompanied by the appropriate payment.
Please make cheques payable to BRF

☐ Please do not send me further information about BRF publications

PROMO REF: QSWILDERNESS
BRF is a Registered Charity

64